To Ann,
Love, Sue

Grandmother's
Treats

Written by Jane Fallon

AVENEL
New York

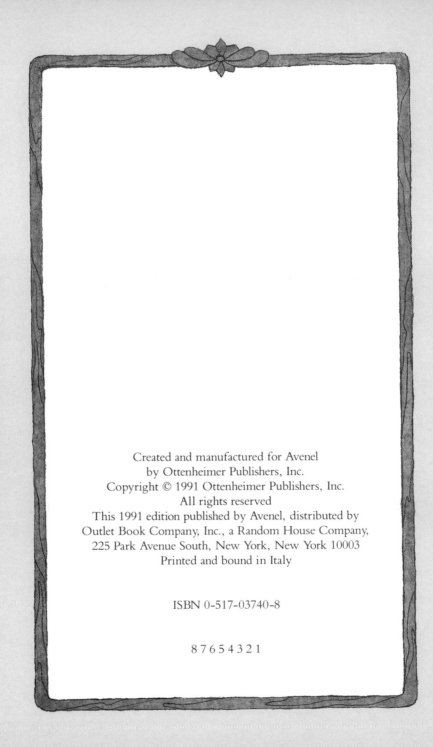

Created and manufactured for Avenel
by Ottenheimer Publishers, Inc.

This 1991 edition published by Avenel, distributed by
Outlet Book Company, Inc., a Random House Company,
225 Park Avenue South, New York, New York 10003
Printed and bound in Italy

ISBN 0-517-03740-8

8 7 6 5 4 3 2 1

Contents

Florentines

Yield: 30 cookies

³/₄ cup raisins
2 cups crushed cornflakes
³/₄ cup peanuts
¹/₂ cup maraschino cherries
¹/₂ can condensed milk
3 ounces sweet baking chocolate

Preheat oven to 375°F. Grease
2 large baking sheets and dust
lightly with cornstarch.

In a large bowl, mix together raisins, cornflakes, peanuts, cherries
and condensed milk. Blend well.
Place 2 teaspoons of mixture in
small heaps on baking sheets. Bake
for 15 minutes. Cool on sheets.

Melt chocolate over a double
boiler, remove from heat, and stir

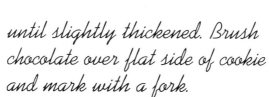

until slightly thickened. Brush chocolate over flat side of cookie and mark with a fork.

Do not store until cookies have completely cooled.

This treasured recipe of my great-grandmother's is passed from generation to generation in our family.

Spice Cookies

Yield: 48 cookies

5 eggs, beaten
2¼ cups firmly packed light
    brown sugar
2 teaspoons cinnamon
1 teaspoon ground cloves
1 teaspoon vanilla extract
1 teaspoon ginger
1 teaspoon baking soda
3 cups flour

Preheat oven to 375°F. Grease baking sheets.

Mix all ingredients in order given above.

Bake for 10 to 12 minutes.

Fudge Brownies

Yield: 32 1-inch squares

2 cups sugar
4 eggs
4 ounces bittersweet chocolate
2 sticks butter
1 1/2 cups flour
1 teaspoon vanilla
1 cup walnuts, chopped

Preheat oven to 350°F.
Beat sugar and eggs together.
Melt the chocolate and butter in a double boiler. Stir the chocolate into the sugar and eggs. Add the flour and vanilla and mix well. Fold in the nuts.
Pour the batter into a 9-inch square baking pan and bake for 1 hour.

Diamonds

Yield: 36 cookies

1 1/2 cups sugar
1/2 cup butter
3 eggs
1 tablespoon water
1 teaspoon vanilla extract
3 cups flour
1 teaspoon baking soda
1/2 teaspoon salt
1/2 cup slivered almonds

Preheat oven to 375°F. Thoroughly grease baking sheets.

Cream the sugar and butter together. Beat in eggs. Add water and vanilla. Stir flour, baking soda, and salt together and stir into batter, mixing thoroughly. Stir in almonds. Refrigerate for 1 hour.

Roll dough ⅛-inch thick on a lightly-floured work surface. Cut into diamond shapes with a sharp knife. Bake for 10 minutes.

The Fourth of July picnic was the biggest annual event in our family, and these cookies were expected to be part of the dessert menu.

Raisin Cookies

2 cups light brown sugar
2 eggs
1 cup vegetable shortening
3 tablespoons sour milk
3½ cups flour
1 teaspoon baking powder
¼ teaspoon baking soda
2 teaspoons cinnamon
1½ cups raisins

Preheat oven to 400°F.

Beat sugar and eggs together until well-blended. Beat in shortening and milk, mixing well. Stir dry ingredients together. Pour into batter and mix thoroughly. Stir in raisins.

Drop by teaspoonfuls onto baking sheets. Bake for 12-15 minutes.

Sugar Cookies

Yield: 60 cookies

2 cups flour
1½ teaspoons baking powder
½ teaspoon salt
½ cup butter
1 cup sugar
1 egg
1 teaspoon vanilla extract
1 tablespoon cream

Sift 1½ cups of flour with baking powder and salt. Cream butter until soft. Beat in remaining ingredients, vanilla, and cream. Stir into the flour. Add enough flour to make dough stiff. Form the dough into a roll and refrigerate.

Preheat oven to 350°F.

Roll dough out on a floured work surface and cut into desired shapes. Bake 10 minutes.

Vanilla Crescents

Yield: 45 crescents

3 cups flour
1 egg yolk
1/8 teaspoon salt
2 tablespoons honey
1 teaspoon vanilla extract
3/4 cup chilled butter, flaked
4 1-ounce squares unsweetened
   baking chocolate

Make a well in the center of the flour and add the egg yolk, salt, honey and vanilla extract. Dot butter over the flour. Using two knives, chop all the ingredients into a crumb texture. Knead quickly to a smooth dough. Form the dough into a roll about 2 inches in diameter and place, covered, in the refrigerator for 1 hour. Preheat the oven to 350°F.

Cut ½ inch thick slices from the roll. Shape into crescents about 2½ inches long and ½ inch thick. Shape into half-moons and place on an ungreased baking sheet. Bake until golden brown. Cool completely.

Melt the chocolate and cool slightly. Dip both ends of the crescents into the chocolate.

Oatmeal Lace Cookies

Yield: 60 cookies

2½ cups quick-cooking oatmeal
1 cup brown sugar
2 teaspoons baking powder
½ cup melted butter
1 egg, beaten

Preheat oven to 350°F. Grease 2 baking sheets.

Stir the oatmeal, brown sugar, and baking powder together. Stir in the melted butter and beaten egg and mix well.

Drop by teaspoonfuls about 1 inch apart on greased baking sheets. Bake for 8 to 10 minutes. Let stand for 1 minute before removing from sheets.

Coconut Cookies

Yield: 48 cookies

4 eggs
5 cups sifted confectioner's sugar
1½ cups flour
3 teaspoons baking powder
1⅓ cups flaked coconut

Preheat oven to 350°F.

Beat eggs until light; add sugar and mix well. Stir in flour and baking powder. Stir in flaked coconut.

Drop by ½ teaspoonfuls on well-greased baking sheets, 3 inches apart. Bake for 10 to 15 minutes.

Store these cookies in a covered jar. Around my house, they never last long enough to get into a jar.

Chocolate Balls

Yield: 40 cookies

3 1-ounce squares unsweetened
  baking chocolate
1 tablespoon strong black coffee
1 cup butter
1/4 cup sugar
1 egg yolk
1 cup chopped walnuts
2 1/2 cups flour
40 walnut halves
Sugar, for coating

Preheat oven to 350°F. Grease
baking sheets.
Melt the chocolate over a double
boiler with the coffee and cool.
Cream the butter and sugar until
light and fluffy. Beat in the egg
yolk. Stir in the nuts and cooled
chocolate. Blend in flour. Chill for
1 hour.

Form teaspoons of the dough into balls, roll well in sugar, and place on baking sheets, leaving space between the balls. Lightly press half a nut into each ball and bake for 15 minutes.

If your family has another kind of nut they prefer, use it in place of walnuts. Cherries are a treat on top of these cookies also.

Butter Cookies

Yield: 60 cookies

⅔ cup butter
¼ cup sugar
2 eggs
3 cups flour
1½ teaspoons salt
2 teaspoons baking powder
1 teaspoon vanilla extract
Sugar, to sprinkle

Cream butter, sugar, and eggs together until light and foamy. Sift dry ingredients together and stir into egg mixture. Stir in vanilla and mix until smooth. Chill for at least 1 hour. Preheat oven to 350°F. Roll chilled dough to ¼-inch thickness on a lightly floured board. Cut into desired shapes, sprinkle with sugar, and bake for 12 to 15 minutes.

Gingersnaps

Yield: 48 cookies

¾ cup vegetable shortening
1 cup brown sugar
¾ cup molasses
1 egg
2¼ cups flour
2 teaspoons baking soda
½ teaspoon salt
1 teaspoon ginger
1 teaspoon cinnamon
½ teaspoon cloves
Sugar, for coating

Preheat oven to 375°F.
Combine shortening, brown sugar, molasses and egg and beat until creamy. Sift dry ingredients together. Add to the creamed mixture and mix well. Form dough into small balls, and roll in sugar to coat. Bake for 10 minutes.

Coconut Cupcakes

Yield: 20 cupcakes

2 cups flour
3½ tablespoons cornstarch
2 teaspoons baking powder
Grated rind of ½ lemon
3 drops lemon extract
¾ cup honey
4 eggs
1½ cups coconut

Preheat the oven to 350°F. Line muffin cups with cupcake liners.

Mix the flour with the cornstarch, baking powder, lemon rind, and lemon extract. Stir in the honey. Stir in the eggs and 1¼ cups of the grated coconut.

Fill muffin cups ¾ full with the batter. Sprinkle with the remaining coconut and bake 15 minutes.

I'm not sure where this recipe came from, but it is one of my favorites. I bake several batches of these cupcakes on Saturday afternoons. Saturday nights my children and their families stop over and always leave with an extra cupcake for everyone.

Black Bottoms

For the cream cheese mixture:
1 8-ounce package cream cheese,
   softened
1 egg
1/3 cup sugar
1/8 teaspoon salt
1 cup miniature chocolate chips
For the cupcakes:
1 1/2 cups flour
1 cup sugar
1/4 cup cocoa
1/4 teaspoon salt
1 teaspoon baking soda
1 cup water
1/3 cup vegetable oil
1 tablespoon vinegar
1 teaspoon vanilla extract

Preheat oven to 350°F. Line miniature muffin cups with miniature liners.

To make the cream cheese mixture, beat together the cream cheese, egg, sugar, and salt. Stir in chocolate chips and set aside.

To make the cupcakes, sift together the flour, sugar, cocoa, salt, and baking soda. Stir in the water, oil, vinegar, and vanilla. Beat well with electric mixer.

Fill muffin cups 1/3 full with the chocolate mixture. Place 1/2 teaspoon cream cheese mixture in each cup. Top with chocolate mixture.

Bake for 15 to 20 minutes.

Orange Cupcakes

Yield: 20 cupcakes

3/4 cup butter

1 1/2 cups sugar

4 eggs, well-beaten

3 cups flour

3 teaspoons baking powder

1/2 teaspoon salt

3/4 cup milk

1 teaspoon grated orange rind

Preheat the oven to 375°F. Line muffin cups with cupcake liners.

Cream the butter and sugar together. Stir in the well-beaten eggs.

Sift the flour, baking powder and salt together and stir into the batter, alternately with the milk. Stir in the grated orange rind. Fill muffin cups 3/4 full with the batter. Bake for 25 minutes.

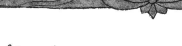

Variations:

For vanilla cupcakes, substitute 1 teaspoon vanilla extract for the grated orange rind.

For chocolate cupcakes, substitute 1 square melted, unsweetened chocolate for the grated orange rind.

Frost cupcakes with your favorite icing.

These cupcakes freeze well, but do not frost before freezing.

Orange Muffins

Yield: 12 muffins

2 cups flour
1 teaspoon soda
1 teaspoon salt
½ cup vegetable shortening
Grated rind of 1 orange
1½ cups buttermilk

Preheat oven to 475°F. Grease muffin cups.

Sift flour, soda, and salt together in a bowl. Cut in shortening until mixture is the consistency of corn-meal. Add grated orange rind, then stir in enough buttermilk to make a soft dough. Place on a lightly floured board and knead lightly. Roll to a ½-inch thickness and cut with a floured round cutter the size of the muffin cups. Place in muffin tins. Bake for 15 minutes.

Apple Muffins

Yield: 12 muffins

2 cups flour
½ cup sugar
1 tablespoon baking powder
½ teaspoon salt
1 teaspoon cinnamon
1 egg
¾ cup milk
¼ cup butter, melted
¾ cup pared, finely chopped
    apple

Preheat oven to 400°F. Line muffin cups with cupcake liners.
Sift together dry ingredients. Beat egg and milk together. Stir in butter. Add to dry ingredients, mixing just enough to moisten. Fold in apple. Fill muffin cups ⅔ full and bake for 20 to 25 minutes.

Blueberry Muffins

Yield: 12 muffins

½ cup butter
1 cup sugar
2 eggs
2 cups flour
2 teaspoons baking powder
½ teaspoon salt
½ cup milk
2 cups fresh or frozen blueberries
1 teaspoon vanilla extract
2 teaspoons sugar

Preheat the oven to 375°F. Line muffin cups with cupcake liners.

Cream the butter and sugar until fluffy. Add eggs, one at a time, and mix until blended.

Sift flour, baking powder, and salt together. Mix into batter alternately with milk. Stir in the blueberries and vanilla.

Fill muffin cups ¾ full with the batter. Sprinkle with sugar. Bake for 30 minutes.

Variations:

Substitute ¾ cup raisings, broken nuts or coarsely cut dates for the blueberries. Stir in with the vanilla.

Cornmeal Muffins

Yield: 8 muffins

½ cup cornmeal
½ cup flour
2 tablespoons sugar
½ teaspoon salt
2 teaspoons baking powder
1 egg, beaten
½ cup milk
2 tablespoons bacon drippings

Preheat oven to 425°F. Grease muffin cups.

Sift cornmeal, flour, sugar, salt, and baking powder together. Stir in beaten egg, milk, and bacon drippings, mixing well.

Fill greased muffin cups ⅔ full with batter. Bake for 15 minutes.

Popovers

Yield: 9 popovers

1 cup milk
1 tablespoon melted butter
1 cup flour
1/8 teaspoon salt
2 eggs

Preheat oven to 450°F. Butter deep muffin cups.

Mix all ingredients except eggs. Add eggs one at a time, beating lightly after each addition.

Fill muffin cups 3/4 full. Bake for 15 minutes, lower heat to 350°F and bake 20 minutes longer. Pierce with a sharp knife to allow steam to escape.

Resist the temptation to peek at these in the oven or they will immediately fall!

Bread Pudding

Yield: 4 servings

1½ cups bread, firmly packed
2 cups milk
3 eggs, lightly beaten
2 ripe bananas, sliced
1 apple, peeled and thinly sliced
½ cup raisins
½ cup sugar
1½ teaspoons cinnamon

Preheat oven to 350°F. Butter a soufflé dish.

Soak the bread in milk for 10 minutes. Mash the mixture and stir in eggs, bananas, apple, raisins, sugar, and cinnamon. Pour mixture into soufflé dish.

Place dish in pan of hot water in oven. Bake until knife inserted in center comes out clean, about 1 to 1½ hours. Cool.

To serve, top pudding with whipped cream.

For Butterscotch Bread Pudding, substitute ½ cup brown sugar for bananas and apples, and proceed with recipe. Serve with milk or any pudding sauce.

Corn Pudding

Yield: 4 servings

½ onion, finely chopped
2 tablespoons butter
1 cup corn kernels
1 tablespoon sugar
Salt and pepper, to taste
3 eggs, separated
½ cup grated cheddar cheese

Preheat oven to 350°F. Grease a
9 x 11-inch casserole pan.

Sauté the onion in butter. Stir in
corn, sugar, salt, and pepper. Cool.
Beat the egg yolks, stir in cheese
and add to the cooled corn mixture.
Beat the egg whites stiff and fold
into the corn-cheese mixture.

Pour into casserole. Set in pan of
hot water and bake for 1 hour.

Serve immediately.

Lemon Pudding

Yield: 4 servings

3 eggs, separated
Rind of $\frac{1}{2}$ orange, grated
Juice of $\frac{1}{2}$ lemon
1 cup sugar
2 tablespoons cake flour
1 cup milk
$\frac{1}{8}$ teaspoon salt

Preheat oven to 350°F. Butter a 1-quart ovenproof casserole dish.

Beat egg yolks and then stir in orange rind and lemon juice. Combine the sugar and flour and add to egg yolk mixture. Stir in milk slowly. Beat egg whites with salt until stiff, and fold into batter.

Pour into greased casserole dish and place in pan of warm water in the oven. Bake the pudding for 45 minutes.

Apple Dumplings

Yield: 6 dumplings

1 1/2 cups flour
1/4 teaspoon salt
1/2 cup vegetable shortening
4 1/2 tablespoons water
6 tart apples, pared and cored
6 tablespoons sugar
3/4 teaspoon cinnamon
3/4 teaspoon butter

Preheat the oven to 425°F. Grease a baking sheet.

Combine the flour, salt and shortening, mixing with two forks until it resembles cornmeal. Stir in the water to form a soft dough.

Roll out and cut into 6-inch squares. Place an apple on each square. Add 1 tablespoon sugar, 1/8 teaspoon cinnamon, and 1/8 teaspoon butter to each apple. Fold the dough around the apples. Prick the dough with a fork and place on the baking sheet.

Bake for 35 to 40 minutes. Serve warm with whipped cream.

For a spicy taste treat, sprinkle the whipped cream with those tiny "red-hots."

Peach Cobbler

Yield: 6 servings

12 fresh peach halves
1/3 cup sugar
2 tablespoons water
1 cup flour
1 1/2 teaspoons baking powder
2 tablespoons butter
1/2 cup milk

Preheat the oven to 450°F.
Place the peach halves on the bottom of a glass baking dish, sprinkle with the sugar and water.
Stir the flour and baking powder together. Using 2 forks, cut in the butter until the mixture resembles cornmeal. Stir in the milk and mix lightly. Spread the dough over the peach halves. Bake for 30 minutes.
Serve warm with cream.

Scalloped Apples

Yield: 6 servings

6 large tart apples
1/4 teaspoon cinnamon
1/8 teaspoon salt
1 tablespoon lemon juice
1/4 cup water
3/4 cup light brown sugar
1/4 cup flour
1/3 cup butter

Preheat oven to 375°F. Butter a
1-quart casserole dish.

Pare, core, and slice the apples.
Place in the casserole and sprinkle
with the cinnamon, salt, lemon
juice, and water.

Mix the brown sugar, flour, and
butter together. Spread this over
the apples and bake for 30 minutes. Serve warm.

Strawberry Shortcake

Yield: 6 shortcakes

1½ cups flour
2 teaspoons baking powder
⅛ teaspoon salt
¼ cup butter
½ cup milk
1½ quarts strawberries, hulled

Preheat the oven to 450°F. Grease
2 baking sheets.

Stir the flour, baking powder and
salt together. Using two forks, mix
the butter into the flour mixture
until granular. Stir in the milk to
form a soft dough.

Roll dough out on a lightly
floured work surface to ¾-inch
thickness. Cut rounds with a bis-

cuit cutter and place on baking
sheets.

Brush the tops of the biscuits with
milk and bake for 12 to 15 minutes.

Crush or slice the strawberries,
setting aside the best whole berries
for garnishing. Sweeten the berries
to taste.

Split each hot biscuit and cover
with the strawberries. Serve with
whipped or table cream, garnished
with whole strawberries.

Cream Puffs

Yield: 10 large puffs

1 cup water
1/2 cup butter
1 cup flour
1/8 teaspoon salt
4 eggs

Preheat the oven to 450°F. Grease 2 baking sheets.

Place the water and butter in a large saucepan and bring to a boil. Mix the flour and salt into the boiling water and beat thoroughly until the mixture begins to leave the sides of the pan and form a ball.

Remove from the heat and add the eggs, one at a time, beating thoroughly after each egg.

Drop by tablespoonfuls on a greased baking sheets. Bake for 20

minutes, the turn heat to 325°F for 20 minutes.

Cool slightly, cut a small opening and spoon out middles. Fill with any desired filling.

Drop cream puff batter from a teaspoon; form tiny cream puffs. Force dough through a pastry tube into eclair shapes.

When baked and cooled, slit one side and full with any custard filling or sweetened whipped cream. Cream Puffs can be frosted with your favorite chocolate icing.

These were a specialty of my grandmother's. She would let me help with the batter and I was always amazed at the way the dough came away from the sides of the pan.

Apricot Balls

Yield: 24 balls

1 cup dried apricots
1/2 cup walnuts
1/2 cup flaked coconut
2 tablespoons wheat germ
4 tablespoons orange juice
1/3 cup finely chopped walnuts

Process apricots, 1/2 cup walnuts, and coconut in food processor. Add wheat germ and orange juice and mix well by hand.

Form into 1-inch balls. Roll in finely chopped walnuts and refrigerate before serving.

Coconut Drops

Yield: 48 drops

1/2 cup semi-sweet chocolate bits
2 tablespoons butter

2 cups confectioner's sugar, sifted
2²/₃ cups flaked coconut
½ cup instant dry milk
1 teaspoon vanilla extract

Grease 2 baking sheets.
Melt chocolate bits and butter over warm water. Blend in the remaining ingredients.
Drop by spoonfuls onto baking sheets. Refrigerate at least 1 hour before serving. Store in an airtight container.

Peanut Brittle

Yield: 1½ pounds

1½ cups peanuts
1½ cups sugar
1½ cups light corn syrup
¼ cup water
2 tablespoons butter
1 teaspoon vanilla extract
1 teaspoon baking soda

Grease a baking sheet with sides or a jelly roll pan.

Place peanuts in a shallow pan and leave them in 200°F oven until warm, not roasted.

Combine sugar, corn syrup, and water in pan. Cook over moderate heat, stirring constantly, until sugar is completely dissolved. Remove any sugar crystals formed above the liquid line. Insert a

candy thermometer and boil the
mixture, without stirring, until
syrup reaches the soft-crack stage
(270°F). Remove from heat.

Add warm peanuts and butter,
stirring well.

Return mixture to the heat. Cook
mixture, stirring frequently, until
thermometer reaches hard-crack
stage (300°F). Remove from heat.

Stir in the vanilla and baking
soda. Mixture will lighten in color
and foam. Pour into pan.

Allow brittle to cool until just
warm to touch then lift the whole
piece with a spatula. Using your
hands, pull and stretch the brittle
to a thin slab. As it cools, you will
be able to break it into small
pieces.

Caramels

Yield: 80 1-inch caramels

1 cup sugar
1 cup light brown sugar
1 cup corn syrup
2 cups heavy cream, lukewarm
½ cup butter, flaked
1 teaspoon vanilla extract
1 cup chopped walnuts

Combine sugars and corn syrup in pan and simmer over low heat, stirring constantly, until sugars are completely dissolved and mixture comes to boil.

Insert a candy thermometer and boil the mixture until the thermometer registers 250°F (hard-ball stage). Add cream very slowly. Cook until temperature reaches 250°F again and add butter, bit by bit. Stir mixture to blend, and bring mixture to 250°F again.

Remove from heat, stir in vanilla and walnuts and pour into lightly oiled 9 x 9 x 2-inch pan. Score caramel in 1-inch squares, but do not cut all the way through.

Cool completely; remove to a cutting board and cut into marked squares. Wrap each caramel in plastic wrap and store in an airtight container.

Grandmother's Nut Candy

Yield: 60 pieces

2 cups honey
1/2 cup sugar
4 cups walnuts, chopped

Lightly oil a 3-quart saucepan. Mix the honey and sugar together in the pan and cook over low heat until boiling. Boil, without stirring, for 10 minutes, stir in nuts.

Insert a candy thermometer and bring mixture to 270°F (soft-crack stage). Pour candy onto a wet work surface. Mixture will be very thick. Pat into square about 1 inch thick. Cut into squares with very sharp knife.

Kisses

Yield: 60 kisses

2 egg whites, room temperature
1/8 teaspoon salt
1/8 teaspoon cream of tartar
1/2 cup sugar

Preheat the oven to 300°F.

Beat egg whites with an electric mixer. Add salt and cream of tartar and continue beating at high speed until egg whites are very foamy and begin to thicken. Add the sugar slowly, beating well after each addition.

When egg whites are very stiff, drop by teaspoonful onto greased baking sheets. Bake 25 minutes.

Turn off oven, open the oven door slightly and cool oven slowly. Remove Kisses from sheets when completely cool.

Turtles

Yield: 60 turtles

1 pound cashew nuts
1 1-pound package caramels
2 tablespoons water
8 ounces semi-sweet chocolate,
  melted

Lightly grease 2 baking sheets. Arrange 60 groupings of cashew nuts, 4 to each group on the sheets. Melt caramels in water in top of double boiler. Cool slightly in pan, but be sure it is still liquid. Spoon tablespoonfuls of liquid caramel over cashew nuts. Cool 10 to 15 minutes.

Spoon melted chocolate over the top of each turtle. Cool until firm.

Try a variation of this delicious recipe:

Substitute 8 ounces butterscotch chips, melted, for the semi-sweet chocolate. Proceed as noted in the recipe.

This candy rivals any store-bought version and satisfies the hungriest sweet tooth.

Potato Fondant

Yield: 2½ dozen eggs

½ cup butter
½ cup warm mashed potatoes
7 cups confectioner's sugar, sifted
1 teaspoon vanilla extract

Blend butter and warm potatoes in a large mixing bowl. Cool completely.

Stir confectioner's sugar and vanilla into cooled mixture, mixing well. Knead until creamy.

Mold into eggs or desired shapes. Chill 1 hour.

Dip in your favorite coating or add coconut; 1½ cups chopped dried fruits; candied fruits; or chopped nuts to this fondant.

To make peanut butter eggs, stir ¾ cup creamy or crunchy peanut butter into mixture before shaping.

Chocolate Fudge

Yield: 1¼ pounds

1⅔ cups sugar
⅔ cup evaporated milk
6-ounces semi-sweet chocolate bits
1½ cups miniature marshmallows
⅛ teaspoon salt
4 tablespoons butter

Grease an 8 x 8 x 2-inch pan.
Combine sugar and milk in a
2-quart saucepan and cook over
medium heat, stirring constantly,
until sugar is completely dissolved
and mixture comes to boil. Boil,
stirring constantly, 5 minutes.
Remove from heat.

Add remaining ingredients. Stir
until chocolate and marshmallows
melt. Beat until thick and not
glossy. Pour into pan. When cool,
cut into squares.

Index

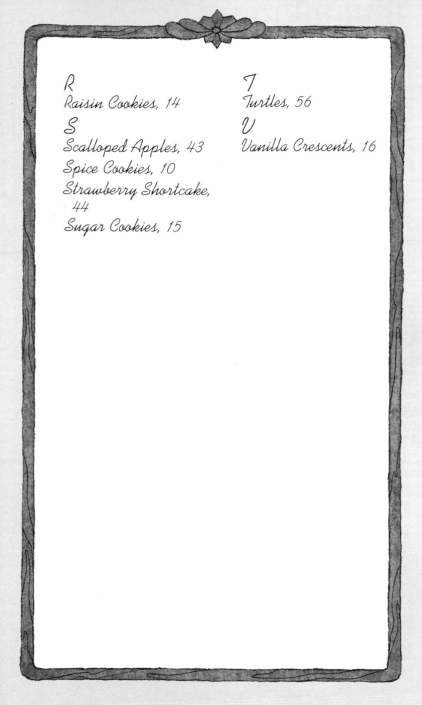

R
Raisin Cookies, 14

S
Scalloped Apples, 43
Spice Cookies, 10
Strawberry Shortcake,
  44
Sugar Cookies, 15

T
Turtles, 56

V
Vanilla Crescents, 16